grow your own Gorgeousness

(seeds included)

By Bethan Stritton

ISBN

9781905493 78

published by

Filament Publishing Ltd
14, Croydon Rd
Waddon, Croydon
Surrey CRO 4PA
Telephone +44(0)208688 2598
info @ filamentpublishing.com
www.filamentpublishing.com
IBSN 978-1-905493-78-4
© 2011 Bethan Stritton

printed by Berforts Group - Stevenage and Hastings
Distributed by Gardners

Thankyou

So far in my Life I have been gifted with knowing some incredible women; all of whom have contributed-perhaps unknowingly- to my personal evolution. Some of these women roar out their Gorgeousness; some are shy; Some recognise their worth; some still don't; some are just working on it. I recognise in all of them a beautiful, unique set of incredible qualities and I want to thank them all for teaching me about true Gorgeousness- especially my mum & K. Fos.

I love you.

Dear ....

Thankyou for being wonderful.

Love from ....

♡ ♡ ♡ ♡ ♡

Contents

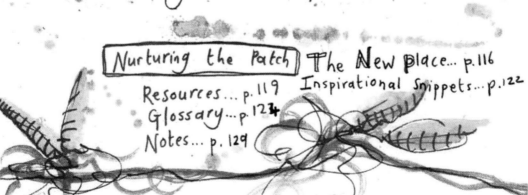

Everlasting Gorgeousness

A long time ago, in the ancient civilization of Atlantis, all women knew the secret of Everlasting Gorgeousness. They did not spend time at the hair dressers. They were not slaves to designer labels and they did not believe that their lives would become complete when they finally fitted into skinny jeans. The women of Atlantis did not need any of these things because they knew.....

no woman has to change her body to become 100% Gorgeous. All she has to do is see how Gorgeous she already is! The moment a woman recognises her own unique style of Gorgeousness a strange and powerful energy is released into the world. When a woman stops resisting and ignoring her own, true Gorgeousness, she suddenly realises how utterly irresistable she is! (sounds simple but so is sliced bread & jam)

This rare, messy, organically cultivated book is about reclaiming your Gorgeousness back again. It's about transcending the twisty turny spaghetti of confusion that we live with and instead shedding our shackles, and practising Radical Self - Expression. It's about rediscovering the unexpected beauty of flawed, imperfect, wonderful human- ness, then getting our hands dirty with the business of living.

This is NOT a personal growth book.

Gorgeousness is not about changing who you are or improving your inner landscape, although you _will_ transform the way you see yourself.

There is no end product to this journey.

Gorgeousness is about being and experiencing not about getting or having.

Also (one last thing): I am not a therapist; I do not have a high media profile; I'm not a practising life coach. I am simply a woman who has had occasional glimpses into Another Way. And I liked it.

                                Because ....

At some point in my childhood I stopped feeling Gorgeous. At some point in lots of peoples lives, they stop feeling Gorgeous as well. We stop trusting that we are lovable and we begin to try and become "good enough to be loved." In my attempts to get love I allowed myself to be led into some situations that now, as an adult, I feel frightened by.

I also learned to see my body as in-adequate, so I made myself sick in an attempt to shrink it down. But as my muscles and my curves shrunk, so did my trust in myself. My sense of well-being became sucked in. I still didn't feel Gorgeous. I felt frail and small. I felt invisible scared, imprisoned, caught, tortured and caged.

Occasionally I would come upon ~~these~~ strange, outrageous women with big eyes, big hair, big hips and big warm love in their hearts and their beauty shimmered around them like golden mists. They accepted themselves

So fully, they expressed their beauty so unashamedly that no-one else around them could possibly deny it. They knew their Gorgeousness

For some time I felt intimidated by these women. I felt angry that they were so free, so strong, so wild and unleashed, while I remained in my cage. But then I began to learn from them and this is what I learnt:-

As women, aunties, godmothers, mums, cousins, sisters and as daughters it is vital that we understand how our lives are controlled by our sense of beauty. Why does research show girls/women feeling too unattractive to be heard; so that they fear asserting themselves? Why have we become so petrified of age/wrinkles that we will inject potentially harmful substances into our faces and chests? We communicate love, fear, affection, compassion, hurt, happiness and joy with our faces, yet we willingly freeze our non-verbal expression. Why? Why? Why? Do we really want to become a race of robot people whose faces are blankly perfect?

Or do we want to feel wild, free, sexy, vibrant, rare, Gorgeously exquisite?

The Dangling
Carrot of Ideal
Beauty - - - -7

We have grown up in the shadow of a great dangling
carrot of ideal beauty. It is dangled from billboards, movies,
advertisments, magazines. It has been estimated that women
today (especially young girls) are exposed to more images of
"ideal beauty" than our grandmothers were in a whole lifetime
Thats enough to make anyone feel insecure about their looks.

12

Who holds up the Dangling Carrot of Ideal Beauty? The Cosmetic companies or US?

Imagine how grumpy all of the cosmetic companies and skin care cream producers and diet manufacturers and exercise DVD sellers and hair straightener makers would be if women learned the truth about "beauty." Imagine the tantrums these people would have if women (and men) learnt to feel gorgeous, trusted in their own delicious magnetism and began to feel equal to the pictures in fashion magazines! Imagine if one day (maybe today) you realized that you are only as attractive as you believe yourself to be and that the only product you need is "to produce more self-love"! ♡ ♡ ♡ ♡

♡ Imagine that!!! ♡ ♡ ♡
♡ ♡ ♡ ♡ ♡
♡ ♡

13

An Impossible Quest

The Dangling Carrot is practically impossible to reach and for those who do reach it, the pleasure never lasts long. When you have slimmed to a size 8, the potential to revert back to size 16 always haunts you. When you have had a nose-job, boob job and teeth veneers, you will inevitably find more imperfections that need fixing. How many years of your life do you intend to squander worrying about your "imperfections"? How many mornings have you woken up to weigh your self-worth on the bathroom scales? The clever inventors of the Dangling Carrot have no interest in you or me attaining Gorgeousness. They simply wait until we are sufficiently hypnotised by wistful aspiration then they get to work selling us creams, lotions, diet pills, make-up, plumping injections, breast implants, acrylic finger nails and shoes with heels like sky scrapers to help women try to

ONE DAY I'LL MAKE IT....
ONE DAY I WILL BE WORTHY...
ONE DAY I'LL ACCEPT MYSELF....
MAYBE...
IF I REACH A STONE.....

reach up and swipe at the Dangling Carrot of Ideal Beauty (somewhere up there - I think......)

14

Throw away your scales and snuggle in an armchair by the window instead. We are bright precious, inquisitive, powerful women. We can choose to turn away from the Dangling Carrot of Ideal Beauty and get some peace or just a cup of tea.

We are Big enough, Bold enough, Outrageous enough to create a brand new place for beauty to sit in our lives. We are Bright enough, Creative enough, Loving enough to begin cultivating our own unique sense of Gorgeousness instead.

A new armchair for Beauty to Rest in!

You can stop buying into the Dangling Carrot of Ideal Beauty and start growing Gorgeousness carrots all of your own.

15

Turning Away

> Quickly! Run away from the carrot while you still can! (it's much nicer where we are)

Turning away from the Dangling Carrot of Ideal Beauty is not always the simplest path to take. While we are following the Beauty Seller's images of "perfection" we are given a goal and we spend out time, life, energy and focus in a quest to reach it. Following the Dangling Carrot is like satellite navigation for your aspiration. (You don't have to think too much).

Choosing to grow your own Gorgeousness means getting off the motorway, tossing your map out of the window and having a picnic in a field under a tree. It means making up your own myths and choosing to love who you are despite the inner criticism, the outer judgement, the misunderstood intentions and resulting arguments, the worry, the fear, the doubt that we stumble over during this life. It is a much nicer place to be than the road to the Dangling Carrot of Ideal Beauty, but it's messier, riskier and you have to make it up as you go along. (meaning engaging our hearts AND brains)

Growing your own Gorgeousness is going Walk-About in the Wilderness with only your trust in{ your Self to sustain you.

Then lying down to watch a butterfly.

Have you ever read a book or watched a film about a person who became lost in the wild, then was liberated through their experience? Sometimes they are helped by an indiginous person and after many adventures they return to "Civilization" but they are (deeply) changed. The person wears a suit again. They wear pointed shoes and dangly earrings but inside their skin they are tangoing, sparking, adventuresome, freshly dancing to the wonder of life.

Choosing to grow your own gorgeousness is actively becoming lost in your own wild, natural self; the liberation and attractiveness that occurs in self-celebration. It's choosing to stop listening to how you "should" be by the sellers of beauty and life style, and allowing your own aliveness to guide you instead.

I believe that in order to break free from the Dangling Carrot trance, we need to discover who we truly are. Digging deep into our soul-soil and discovering our inner treasures, our unique callings, our inspirations, our myths and our stories is what will lead us back to our unquantifiable self.

This may require some flamboyant gardening gloves!

For so long the Dangling Carrot of Ideal Beauty has lured us. It's led us down the garden path, out of the gate, under the hedge and onto the crazy Beauty Highway. (It is a very busy place!)

We have been on this highway for a long, long time. The idea of leaving can be a frightening prospect. After all, what will saying "No!" to the Dangling Carrot actually mean for us women? Will we end up as chronically obese yeti types? Exactly what will we be surrendering if we start to love our bodies just as they are?

These fears show us what a slim tightrope we are balancing on.

We are petrified of being punished with ugliness if we dare defy the Dangling Carrot standards. We cringe at the feeling of being less-than-enough so much that we'd rather spend a life time battling our own bodies. We've been taught/hypnotised that reaching the Dangling Carrot will bring us love and success, and deviation our downfall. We've been so misled.

It is time to return to our gorgeous selves!

new way (take at own risk)

I don't know what it will mean to turn away from the Dangling Carrot of Ideal Beauty, but I am prepared to find out. And I'm not alone. All over the world, rare, spirited, wildly daring women are being called upon to wake up from the dangling carrot trance. These women are trampling out new pathways. They are creating new ways of seeing. They are brewing new perspectives.

new perspectives
new perspectives

I believe that if this book has found you and its message resonates with your heart, then you are being called onto the path of gorgeousness.

The rest of this book contains my offering to you. It could be seen as a stick like the ones that gardeners use to support broad beans as they grow big and abundant. (you are a gorgeous bean, yes you are!!!)

Or it could be seen as a potting shed full of tools, bulbs, inventions and creative explorations to help your gorgeousness thrive. You can read through these practises one by one or you can cherry-pick the ones that appeal to you most. These tools are now yours. Use them however you like.

raking the soil

The purpose of this chapter is to reconnect you with your body & feelings - exactly as you are right now.

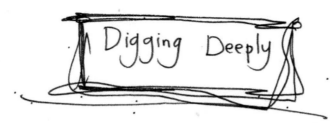

Digging Deeply

Remember being little and going out into the garden to dig? All you needed was a spade, a dream of lost treasure and a sense of adventure.

&

When my brother and I went digging, we always headed to a spot at the bottom of the garden where the ground was squashy and rich. Sometimes we dug for diamond rings, sometimes for pieces of broken china or lost clay pipes. Other times we dug for Australia.

Years later, after the death of my father and my brother's murder, I went to see a counsellor and began a new excavation. I found...

ⓐ Sparkling treasure
ⓑ Lost memories
ⓒ Broken bits of grief, loss, pain
ⓓ Self judgement
ⓔ More self judgement - especially around my body, my actions and my short comings.

I realized how many of my actions, time & energy were used to cover up these parts of myself or fix the flaws I was so desperate to hide.

I wore a smile that felt like a mask ~~and~~ and behind it I was all tangled up.

Inside all of us are treasures and diamonds and strange ways and beautiful means. There are also repressed emotions, old memories left undigested, fear, guilt, emptiness. These are the bits and bobs many people would rather leave hidden. Yet only by digging deeply, unearthing these objects and holding them tenderly, can we let them go. We can stop judging and hiding and instead feel the soft, sighing, crumbling peace of self acceptance. We can rest on the soft, fertile soil that is us, no longer fearing the prod of self denial and look up at the stars instead.

* The soft soil of a soul who has fallen in love with herself is a very comfortable bed to snuggle in.

For many years I was petrified of what lay beneath my surface. I tried to ignore, and shove down my wild, feeling Bethan-ness. Just like I tried to hide and sculpt parts of my body so they'd be acceptable, I believed that certain feelings and dreams should be taped up and thinned down too. I perceived that society didn't like anything too feeling-full, too loud, too real, too colourful or vivid.

My feelings were rather like my body's twin sister - equally difficult to contain and keep in order. However, my feeling side was more fiery than her twin and that part of me wouldn't stay taped down for long.

Like the Hindu goddess Kali who dances on Lord Shiva, all of my lost cont-inents of pain and anger and suppression would rise up. Enraged, they would lash out on an unsuspecting husband, surprised white van drivers and undeserving shop assistants... especially during phases of PMT.

26

DANGER -
woMan in
Process

I admit that it was quite dangerous to be
around me at times. And still can be!

Yet through all this twisty, turny adventure
into my deep self, I learned that nothing
is "good" or "bad". Feelings, bodies and our
understanding of the World (wherever we
are standing) simply ARE. They need our
love as much as our goodness, compassion &
godliness. I learned that we little humans
are bigger, more complex and more profound
than a vast continent. We are bursting with
joy, cruelty, courage, weakness, tenderness, aching
love and bitter hatred. We are urban
sophisticates, cold tyrants, bohemian travellers
and back-stabbing villains. We are Everything,
Good and Bad, mixed up in a gorgeous vessel
of Flesh & Blood.

And that is perfectly perfect!

27

As we let our
own light shine,
we subconsciously
give other
people permission to
do the same.

– Marianne
    Williamson

For us to grow our gorgeousness, we need to learn to accept _all_ _of_ _our_ _parts_. That includes the aspects in us that we find ugly, raucous or wild. This does not mean that we can't develop or evolve the uncomfortable areas. In fact often when we accept and surrender to those aspects rather than resisting them, they seem to just melt away.

Can you accept your self just as you are right now?

Can you embrace the whole - you?

We can ease ourself gently into self acceptance by asking ourselves: little questions like:-

What lies beneath the surface of my smile? Do I have feelings hidden deep inside me that I daren't admit to anyone?

Am I open and caring and kind to myself when a negative feeling emerges or do I make quick get-aways into the

⊚ biscuit tin? ⊚ wine? ⊚ _ _ _ _ _ _ _ _ _ ?

(fill in your favoured method of feeling escape)

EXIT here

biscuits

Run u!

What do I fear most about expressing my true self?

It takes vast daring and courage to look at, who we are and witness our (Whole)someness. It is so easy to shove down and ignore great chunks of our truth. Asking these very questions allows us to stand on the brink of our truth. The next step

is to lean in further by beginning
an :-Enquiry-:

Enquiry is giving our body language
and our true feelings a voice. It
is an ancient communication—with—
whole-self technique that was used by
the wild women of Atlantis. Today's
women tend to judge a feeling as good
or bad and depending on how good it
makes us feel we either seek more
or make a quick get-away.

How often do we pause to let our
feelings actually speak?

Enquiry lets our feelings communicate
with us through metaphor, imagery
and senses so we can work through
them & then let them go.

31

How to have a Creative Enquiry

① Three times a day pause and ask yourself "how do I feel in my body right now? Does this feeling have a colour? What shape is this feeling? If this feeling was some weather, what sort would it be?"

② Continue to track the feeling. Has it changed size, location or colour? Has it evolved into a new feeling?

③ Keep on observing your feeling until it melts away. Otherwise find someone with magical listening ears and tell them about your feeling and where it sits inside you. You can use the cards on the following pages to document & collect your Enquiry findings.

begin the

Enquiry

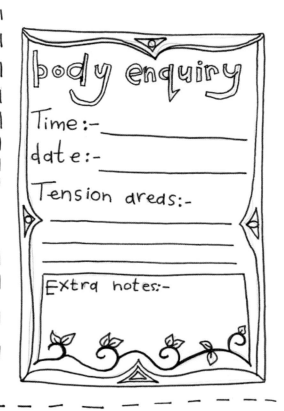

body enquiry

Time:-

date:-

Tension areas:-

Extra notes:-

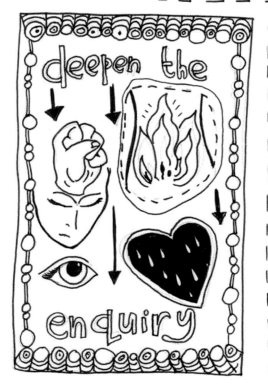

deepen the

enquiry

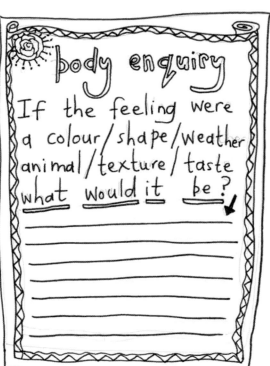

body enquiry

If the feeling were a colour/shape/weather animal/texture/taste what would it be?

Enquiry COLLection   DATE:-

"Just for today I will pause and explore my feelings and collect them kindly." signed _____

① _____

② _____

③ _____

④ _____

⑤ _____

⑥ _____

⑦ _____

At the end of today I felt like this:-

Emergency Enquiry Method

There is a special sort of
Enquiry that you can do when
you are flooded with an
uncomfortable feeling such as
anger, shame, guilt, upset,
insecurity, worthlessness or panic.
I discovered / invented this method
in a hotel room in Maderia
after a terrible argument that
had left me confused, shaken,
shocked and upset.
What I loved about this Enquiry
is that it peels back your outer
defence feelings and reveals your
truth, hence restoring you to gorgeousness.

When you are feeling ugly, brutish, clumsy, stupid, pathetic, weak, incapable, apathetic, hairy fat, monstrous or however you feel when you are lying in a pit of self judgement, take a blank piece of paper and draw yourself. You may look like a blob or a speck, or a strange, lumpy alien. Draw how disgusting/rubbish you feel then write a list of all the negative, squelchy thoughts, feelings and self judgements beside your picture. Now, without thinking about it, quickly draw a creature coming from the top (perhaps the head) of your drawing. The new creature could be an insect. You could even draw a fruit or a vegetable. It doesn't matter. Be free. Just draw. Now make a list of how you would describe this little creature / thing. What does it like? What does it need? What is it's attitude to life? Compare this creature / thing to your first drawing. How different are they? Are they connected? Is the second picture a truer representation than your first drawing? Play with this.

36

Once when I discovered this exercise
I drew a great blobby, lumpy thing that was
clumsy, unelegant, loud and obnoxious. Perched
on it's head was a tiny beetle who just wanted
to mind it's own business, live simply and not get
squashed. This beetlish part of me was/is frightened of big feet.

Help!
help!

This part of my Self
tries to protect itself by behaving
in clumsy, unelegant, loud, obnoxious,
ways. The beetle turns into
an ogre when it feels frightened
and vunerable. Sometimes we
judge our Selves when we don't
even understand ourselves. We are horribly,
incredibly, mysterious, multi-dimensional beings. We all
have ogres, She-Wolves, beetles, carrots, Electrical Eels,
spiders of creation and Vampires in Our characters.
They are all there to try and help you survive
one way or another. Dig down. Rake the soils.
Study what you discover. Throw out your judgement.
Love your freshly uncovered soul.

37

Being Willing to feel Gorgeous

When we make Enquiry a daily habit it quickly becomes clear that we are _not_ our feelings. Yet feelings add so much flavour to our lives!

We learn that feelings can't be escaped but they can be listened to, felt and worked through. Feelings - and our pursuit of gorgeous feelings - fan us in many directions. It is the promise of delicious wholesome feelings that keep us chasing the Dangling Carrot and fear of bad, ugly feelings that imprisons us in this Ideal Beauty Quest. Use the next page to list all of the wondrous, luxurious feelings you have imagined you would feel if you could achieve your idealized self.

A spice rack of feelings.

If I looked exactly how I
long to look, I'd feel....

how?
loved?
respected?
successful?
worthy?
good enough?
happy?
joyful?
at peace?

(tell the page!)

Have a read of your list. Study those wonderful, nutritious, juicy feelings and ask yourself this:

Am I willing to allow myself to feel these feelings right now just as I am?

Your willingness to feel good without having to do more, be more, diet more, obsess more can feel **really** scary. Its almost like stepping bare footed in nature after years of tottering about in 6 inch heels. As this tiny seed ☀-of possibility to feel good - yes just as you are! - emerges, all sorts of jumpy thoughts and feelings will clamour for your attention.

You will be filled with a multitude of reasons why you can't, mustn't, shouldn't, couldn't, wouldn't possibly be able to feel gorgeous just as you are. This is utterly normal & to be expected. Capture these jumpy fears right here so they can be explored. you can wear an explorers hat!

If I began to feel gorgeous & love/accept myself just as I am, I might:-

get fat? Achieve nothing? Be ugly?
have awful skin? Die alone?

If I begin to feel gorgeous & love/accept myself just as I am, other people will:—

Laugh? Look down on me? Reject me? Not love me?

If I surrender to my wondrous self I might have to:—

change? take scary steps? let go of dysfunctional relationships?

The answers to these questions start to unearth your deepest fears and inadequacies. They are the trapped feelings that have become wedged in your soul soil and need to be explored tenderly if you are to remove them.

These deep, hardened feelings are pollutants to your gorgeousness. They need to be explored, enquired into and released in healthy ways.

You could:-

◎ Write a letter to yourself promising that what ever happens you will always be loved by you. ♥

◎ explore ways to shift blocked emotions such as E.F.T or counselling sessions

◎ Read & work through John Bradshaw's book "Homecoming" and reclaim and reparent the aspects of you that are hurting and fearful.

Watering your patch

(of gorgeousness carrots)

100% purified, raw, crystalish, diamond natural gorgeousness

gush warble warble whisper burble burble whisper bubble wonder wonder
flow nag chitter chatter nag churn gush flow whisper

The purpose of this chapter is to explore your inner conversation and end the self-talk that prevents you from accessing your true gorgeousness.

tut

chatter   whitter   on & on

chat   warble   warble   you should

                              gush   on & on   whisper

nag   whisper lurble.   you mustn't

                                                        chatte

Introducing the
Beauty Conversation

It is no surprise that women today have entire compost heaps full of fear around "not being good enough." No one is 100% free.

Just because I'm writing/creating this book does not mean I am free of the Dangling Carrot of Ideal Beauty.

One minute I'll be humming a tune & watering my gorgeousness carrots, then the next minute I'll see something on t.v and Vhuum I'm back on the motorway traipsing after

Watering the patch

the perfect body
and berating myself
for not being a
size 8. However,
since I woke up
once to the Dangling
Carrot, now I find I
can wake up again,
& again & again.

I can remind myself
who I truly am, get back onto the
path of my gorgeousness and shift
my thinking away from the Dangling
Carrot.

few people realise how power-<u>full</u>
our thinking is.

Our self talk ~ this mental dialogue
we have with ourselves ~ is the very
water that can feed our gorgeousness
or keep it stunted in the dark.
Our thinking leads us away from our
gorgeousness & it can also lead us back again.

47

And most of us, unless we are exceptionally oblivious to the culture we live in, have had our self-talk utterly saturated by the Dangling Carrot Conversation. Ideal Beauty conversations are pouring from T.V shows, book shelves billboards, pop songs, car branding & family conversations around farmhouse tables. Like a river in the background of our lives this conversation has rushed, gushed, thundered and burbled the Dangling Carrot myths. This background noise has become so acceptable that it is whispered wherever we go. We hardly even notice it anymore.

There comes a point when this outer beauty conversation becomes an inner one. It is as though a river of self-judgement and Ideal Beauty Whisperings flow through us... rushing, gushing, burbling and that is when the Dangling Carrot has snared us.

- Once this has happened how is it possible to become free of the Dangling Carrot conversation and scramble back onto the riverbank of gorgeousness again?
- How do we bend our rigid perceptions BACK into the natural gorgeous postures & perceptions that fill us with rich grace?

49

A Jar/tool

Most of us are aware of the thundering river of beauty conversations in our outer lives. Now become aware of the beauty conversation within your own mind. ↘

Begin a collection of Inner Transcripts that capture your Dangling Carrot Conversation river water in a jar. To do this is simple: just buy a thick pad and resiliant pen. Then each morning for three weeks, get up and write three pages of WHATEVER comes into your mind.

You will be amazed at how much stuff your mind can churn out. Don't try and come up with things...

50

... just let everything you think of pour out onto the page. Keep going for three whole weeks, stashing your gorgeousness pages☀①in a safe place until you're done.

This may seem like a bizarre project, however these gorgeousness pages are perfect for exploring your Ideal Beauty conversation that goes on <u>all the time</u> in your brain. In these pages you will discover your guilt at "not being good enough", your resolve to "improve" or "get back" to the rose-tinted body you owned age 17. You'll discover your boredom, your grittiness, your tender hopes and gradually you'll notice one particular voice that dominates your Ideal Beauty Conversation.

① adapted from Morning pages - The Artist's Way by Julia Cameron

This loud voice belongs to your

Inner Judge
(loud speaker)

It is your Inner Judge that makes you feel like you are under Beauty Surveillance. "Don't get fat, don't get wrinkles, hide your flesh, scrub at the cellulite, keep hands looking young, refuse to...)

The Inner Judge **demands** obedience to the Dangling Carrot of Ideal Beauty. He/she encourages you to become fixated on "fat or thin", "light or heavy," "lined or flawless", "good or bad", "ugly or beautiful." Your Inner Judge smiles and nods approvingly when we meet Dangling Carrot standards but shrivels us with revulsion if we don't.

Shine the light on the voice of your Inner Judge through your gorgeousness pages.

52

People who have very powerful, LOUD Inner Judges seem to hate this book. They despise the message of flawed, rare gorgeousness and sometimes have wanted to burn it at the stake!

Gorgeousness threatens the Inner Judge because it gives us back our freedom. It restores our power to make Real Choices about who we want to be. These choices reflect our True self worth, our value as unique individuals and our natural power to create gorgeous life experiences. It is now time to begin an adventurous new conversation with yourself. This time the old Ideal Beauty record will be turned down & a dialogue of gorgeousness will unfold. Are you ready?

Firstly Look through your gorgeousness pages and pluck out all of your most common Inner Judge snipes, such as: "I'm too short, I'm dumpy, I have huge calves etc."

⊙ Now use those judgements to make a hilarious piece of art which reflects how your Inner Judge sees you. You could paint yourself, draw yourself, sculpt yourself in pottery or create a costume. It doesn't matter if you don't believe yourself to be an artist.

This piece of Art is Expressionism... And we are all Expressionists!

⊙ Maybe, if it's not too scary you could make a doll that represents the way you've seen yourself. There are many types of dolls... paper dolls, rag dolls, wooden dolls, wire dolls....

◉ Once your art is complete, look at it. Is this really how you are? What do you want to do with your art now? Would you like to bury it? Hug it? Or would

54.

you like to get rid of it? Could you add to it? Reshape it? Make it differently? Note what you'd like to do with your piece of Art right here ↓

What does your answer tell you about how you feel towards your Inner Judge and the remarks he/she says?

Now do whatever you like to your Art and know that this is perfectly OK.

Secondly, tell your Inner Judge to "Leave Now".

This may sound simplistic, however, it's vital that you recognise that the Inner Judge Is Not You. It may speak with your voice and sound like you, but it is just the Ideal Beauty conversation internalised in your mind.

You can turn that voice off by telling the Inner Judge to leave.

Does this sound hard to believe? For many years I refused to believe it. Then, one day I became exhausted with telling myself I wasn't enough. I was so jaded with waking each morning, feeling my stomach to see how jutty-outy my hip bones were, then resolving to begin another new diet.

That day I turned to the picky, on-going nagging voice in my head and said, "I have had enough. Leave now."*

And guess what happened?

The Voice went quiet. I think it was shocked. I was shocked. I felt like Celie in Alice Walkers book "The Color Purple" when she tells Mister that she is leaving with Shug.

The whole of my inner-space fell into Shocked Silence. For the first time in my whole life I realised that I really could turn off the Inner Judge... simply by recognising that a) it was not me and b) I could instruct it to get out of my thought river and it would leave.

* My actual words weren't "leave now". One began with "f" and the other "o." It was rude and sweary and angry, but that was the truth about how I felt.*

57

give your Inner Judge an Image

By giving your Inner Judge an image, you can **separate** yourself from it even further. I imagined the voice to be a thin, pointed finger with a sharp accusing nail that was perpetually prodding at me to:- "lose more weight, diet harder, look better, exercise more."

Once you have given your Inner Judge an image, write a letter to it. Tell it, in no uncertain terms, to LEAVE. Officially un-invite the Inner Judge. Tell it everything... how it has made you feel through the years, the things you've done to appease it's nagging. Tell it that you are no longer being party to the Dangling Carrot of Ideal Beauty conversation and from now on, you will be growing your own gorgeousness instead. Now sign your letter, take it into your garden/local park and light it with a match.

Watch as your Inner Judge goes up in flames

Now make
ted

Take time
To feel
How it feels
To be free Of
the Inner Judge's
CLAMBOURING
demands
Sit with yourself. And rest
In the peaceful knowingness
Of
I am ok. I am Enough.
And that is Enough.

60

Then thirdly.......

choose a sprinkling of these gorgeousness affirmations and add them to your Inner Conversation. Invite them in like new friends. Let these affirmations dissolve into you, like organic miracle growth pellets and begin to feel your gorgeousness stir.

I trust in myself. I respect my needs & boundaries

Each day I travel to glorious new places within myself.

I am a vessel of gorgeous gifts.

I can easily find pathways to let out my dreams & visions

I am perfectly acceptable just as I am.

I am ready to let planet Earth

I allow my Truth to guide me.

I see me in my true gorgeousness

I experience my body as a temple for my gorgeousness

My happiness and self worth is the doorway to true beauty

61

Other Ways To Water Your Carrots

◉ Take your list of negative self judgements from page 54 and turn them into positive statements instead. For example "I am boring and dull" can be recreated into "I am bursting with life, treasure and rich gifts for the world." OR "I am a strange shape... all out of proportion," could be repainted as "I am perfectly gorgeous just as I am."

◉ At first new, positive self talk can feel alien and uncomfortable (a little like learning Yoga postures when you have never done it before). Don't let this put you off! Say these positive statements <u>all the time.</u> Get used to them. Feel how it would feel if you <u>truly</u> believed them.

◉ Make believe your gorgeousness! I used to ~~When~~ struggle hard to see myself as a "real" writer and the more I struggled to become one, the <u>less</u> I could access my creativity. When I was small I had no trouble writing and this was partly because I was so relaxed about the whole thing. I would simply <u>pretend</u> I was a writer and the more I pretended, the more writing I would do. I was _so_ happy the day that my mum & dad bought me a bureau for then, I felt, my dreams of being a writer were really coming true. Now, when I have problems with writer's block or I doubt my abilities, I simply go to my bureau and pretend to be a writer just like I did when I was little. When we make believe in ourselves, we are free to become that person.

Releasing your raw, delicious gorgeousness is the same. Say your affirmations to yourself. Summon the feeling of "I AM GORGEOUS" up from your belly. Go about your tasks, your chores, your daily life make-believing that this is you.

because it 100% truly is.

planting
the seeds

The purpose of this
chapter is to assist you
in experiencing
your gorgeousness in
a brand new and
very real way.

"I have crossed an ocean,
I have lost my tongue,
from the root of the old one,
a new one has sprung."

— Grace Nichols
(The Fat Black Woman's Poems)

By becoming aware of your thought river and by choosing to affirm/love/embrace your exquisite self, you become the source of your gorgeousness. Beauty scarcity becomes a thing from yesterday. The Dangling Carrot of Ideal Beauty loses its power over your sacred gorgeousness and you gradually feel your way into a new life experience.

Does this seem possible to you yet?

OR is it still too tempting to think that life & you are set in stone? Are you thinking, "if I am not gorgeous NOW, how will I ever be.... especially with time and youth slipping away day by day? To break these fears and turn our lives and gorgeousness around we have to understand what the wild women of Atlantis knew:- "life" is not set in stone.

Life is a strange, vibrant, sometimes painful, sometimes achingly sweet

Experience

of our self and 'Planet' Earth. (An) (experience) that we dance through & create each and every day. And all experience is transformationable. (New words are sometimes required)

Take a few moments to imagine this....
....You wake up and look in the mirror
to discover you are having a less-than-
gorgeous day (experience of yourself/body).
You get dressed but even your best
clothes and flawless make-up fail to cover
your scrawny feelings of "not-enoughness."
You head off to work, scuttle down
the highstreet, pausing for a moment
to glance at the work of a street
artist as she chalks flowers onto the
pavement. In that moment the artist
looks up and quickly she captures your
face in chalk. She smiles up at you &
says, "you have the most worldly
soulful eyes I have ever seen.
I just had to capture
      them here."

You know that the artist is
sincere. Happiness floods through
you and continuing on your way
you are suddenly filled with poise,
grace, radiance and a sense of
deep value.

Has your life changed? No.
Your experience of yourself
and life has changed. experience
oil paints

When we begin to view our Experience
of life, our bodies, our work and our relationships
as something that we can shift at any
time, we become artists of our daily life.
We stop wandering through our days like beggars,
starved of gorgeousness, asking that our bodies, faces
and roles validate who we are. We no longer
need to scavenge around for a few
worthiness pennies to grace our bowl.
Instead we tango through our Earth
Experience like gorgeous,
radiant goddesses.

Up until this time the Dangling Carrot of Ideal Beauty has cunningly manipulated our experience of the body and the self.

It has encouraged division.

It has made body hatred common practise. It has fragmented our gorgeousness & self worth.

So wily

The Dangling Carrot has done this by manipulating our focus.

And (paintbox)

Our experience is created by what we choose to focus our attention on. Really!

Let me give you an example of how this works...

Look around the room and count how many red things you can see.

Do that now.

Okay... now write here → [____] how many blue things you saw. If you didn't cheat, you won't be able to! That is because you were (focusing) on looking for red and so reddishness was what came into your experience.

What do you think you will experience if you go looking for your ~~flaws~~ body flaws?

Through clever advertising and media and branding and images upon

images
upon
images upon
images

of one limited version of "ideal beauty", our focus is drawn again & again to the places where we don't add up. Our minds are guided towards our imperfections.

This has resulted in a daily experience of imperfection.

We can RADICALLY alter our experience of our bodies by choosing to shift our (focus) towards our gorgeousness rather than our "flaws". We can grow fresh perspectives, new ways of seeing & new born eyes.

I have grown to LOVE experimenting with my life Experience.

The most rebellious, daring, raucous way I've found to radically shift out of the Dangling Carrot mindset is to ACTIVELY ACKNOWLEDGE the gorgeousness.

The more we can practise this, the more we experience it, the more we believe it & the more we generate it. Eventually this builds to a point of critical mass. Our experience of our gorgeousness infuses everything we do, say & create, and even other peoples' experience of us is transformed.

you mean others will see me differently?
how can this be?

It is believed that only 10% of what we communicate to others is expressed in words. Another 30% is expressed in the sounds we make. A miraculous 60% is conveyed with our body language. Our postures & stances *display* who we believe / experience ourselves to be. The way we walk, talk, smile, look at people, sit down, stand up, leave a room & enter it, all subconsciously tell people who we are and how we Experience ourselves.

Our bodies talk!

75

When we doubt our gorgeousness and choose to Experience our bodies as less-than-enough, our energy shrinks back as if we are trying to make ourselves invisible.

✗

However, when our gorgeousness is blooming and we experience great bursts of self celebration, we are magnetic. We have presence. We become fountains of gorgeousness Our bodies walk tall, our shoulders are thrust back, we smile deliciously and welcome in the world. In other words, other people cannot help to experience our gorgeousness too.

There are many
WAys to actively Acknowledge
the gorgeousness
(and reclaim your focus back again)

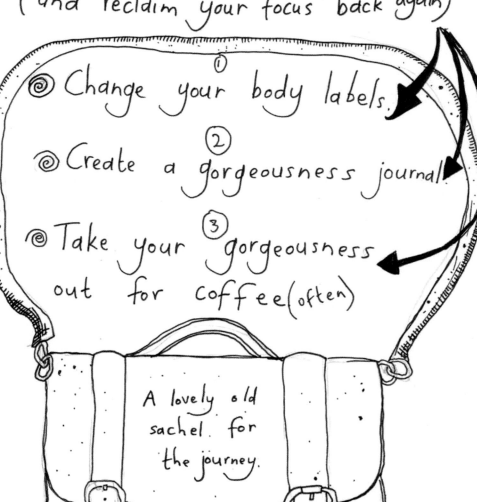

① ◎ Change your body labels.

② ◎ Create a gorgeousness journal

③ ◎ Take your gorgeousness
out for coffee (often)

A lovely old
sachel for
the journey.

body labels

I am fat!

I am short!

my thighs are too big!

I have no breasts!

In my late teens I fitted the Ideal Beauty mould. I was "thin" enough, "bony enough," I had the right clothes, the right hair and I was also more miserable than I've ever been in my life.

The cost of the prize was high. On the outside I looked how many women long to look but on the inside I felt worse than I did when I was a chubby little girl being bullied. The strange thing was this:- even though I slotted into 90% of the Dangling Carrot Ideal, there was always <u>something</u> that still

Tags hanging on a line:

My arms are hairy!

I have too many bumps!

My tummy has stretch marks!

My ears stick out!

Wasn't quite right. Okay I was slim - but now I had no boobs!! It was Endless.

People would say "just accept yourself as you are", but how could I love and accept what I saw as unacceptable?

I was so acutely aware of the cultural conversation around

perfect = acceptable / loved
imperfect = not good enough/unloved

and the battle was exhausting.

I needed to find a new way - a new (peace) - with my self.

and the journey began. It started with something very simple:- language

I discovered that the way we choose to use language and label ourselves is one of our most powerful tools. By naming something we give it life. We give it form.

In many ancient cultures people would not share their true names as they believed this gave another person power over them

80

In many companies & businesses, people have realized the power of names and labelling. "Problems" have become "challenges" because a challenge is so much easier to solve.

How we name a thing transforms how we (see) it.

We can choose to name our bodies "fat" or "abundant".

We can name a part of us "ugly" or "distinctive".

And as we choose juicy, delicious positive language to describe our beautiful bodies, we will begin to experience them in a juicy, delicious new way.

81

An ✦exploration✦ into your Body Labels

Pick out some of the body names below,
think about the part of your body this
relates to. Let your reactions and conditioned
labels reveal themselves... positive & negative.

belly

nails

lips

hands

feet

eyelashes

HAIR

fingers

thighs

neck

Skin

Arms

ankles

legs

back

face

nipples

eyes

vagina

shoulders

calves

knees

Ears

bottom

hips

breasts

nose

We label ourselves so easily. We have negative labels hanging off our bodies from the moment we begin doubting our Gorgeousness.

Here are some of my labels....... →

that I have believed when I didn't understand my own unique Gorgeousness.

hair not straight enough

cheeks too red
eyes too narrow
eye-brows too thick
hair line too low

shoulders too broad.

chest too flat

arms too thick

stomach too flabby

hands like a builders

thighs wobbly

legs - stumpy

83

It's almost impossible not to label ourselves, but we can consciously choose to use different words. Here is how I renamed my body; (starting from the bottom up - legs that is).

Legs - strong, resiliant, powerful springboards into worldly adventures

Thighs - smooth, soft, warm, strokable, comfortable

Hands - practical, empowered with creation, artistic, sculpturistic, loyal, natural, builders of dreams,

Stomach - bearer of life, tatooed with small silver fish/moonbeams from cradling my babies

Arms - quick as lightening, strong like a Goddess, full of power, protection, weight-bearing, independent.

Chest - small but perfect, lets me run fast and read lying down; cute, capable, mine.

Shoulders - strong, powerful, could carry a basket of luxurious fruit through a desert but wouldn't tire.

Cheeks - earth natural, Eyes - feline Eyebrows - perfectly sculpted Hair-line - Just don't get a fringe.

Hair - Natural, frenzied, wild, bushy, thick, bohemian

Write a list of your negative body labels, then change the words. Redefine and refine your perception (make "you" mean "Gorgeous", "Gorgeousness"...

Now it is :your: turn!

You can use the next two pages to alter, rewrite and become creative with the language you use to describe yourself.

Take each body label that you collected (page 76) and then spend some time redefining & refining your perception of gorgeousness.

Your task:- Make "gorgeousness" mean you exactly as you already are.

Capture your new labels here...

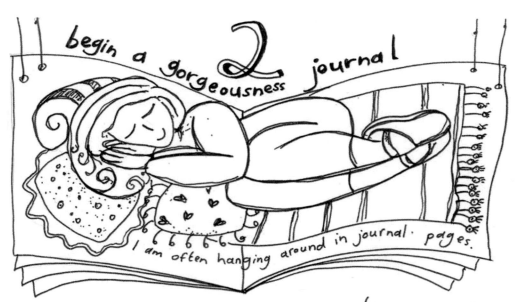

begin a gorgeousness 2 journal

I am often hanging around in journal pages.

growing gorgeous perspectives and seeing your body through fresh eyes will take time. It is a process that we must commit to if we are to limber up the stiff mindset that the Dangling Carrot of Ideal Beauty has produced. It is a process of urging, shifting, remembering to go within and deliberatly choosing to focus on the gorgeousness in yourself and others.

Another great way of actively acknowledging the gorgeousness (and hence drawing it into your life-of--experiences) is to keep a gorgeousness Journal. Each night before you go to sleep, simply sit and list 7 things that you appreciate about your body or yourself. What begins as "just a list" grows into a gorgeousness generator. With each list a new habit is formed, you will naturally become drawn to all of the juicy, wonderful, lovable aspects of yourself and powerful gorgeousness perspectives will emerge.

You could buy a thick sumptuous book to use as a journal or turn to the next page & find instructions to make your own. I do believe that when we D.I.Y with books & journals they become infused with the power of our creativity.

Gorgeousness Journal

You will need...

(this stuff is all easily getable from art & crafty shops)

a sheet of A1 grey board

24 sheets of A3 cartridge paper (140g if you can)

pencil pen

PVA glue

strong needle & thread.

sellotape

scrap paper

50 cm of ribbon

ruler

Craft knife

glue brush

scissors

100% cotton for covering

enthusiasm jam

Warming beverage

Some really HEAVY books to act as weights.

and now....

1

2

B ← - - - - → A

Divide your pages into sets of 4. Fold in half then insert into each-other.

place your book sections on top of eachother next to the edge of a table.

3 Make a pencil mark 15 mm in from either end of the book.

4 Divide the space between the pencil marks into 3. For example

1   2   3

5.

Cut three pieces of ribbon, place them _over_ the 3 pencil marks and tape ribbon onto the table edge.

6

Next get your bit of scrap paper and make sure it is the same length as the sections. Fold in half and line up the folded edge with your book. Mark where the ribbons + "pencil mark A" sit.

Take each section of your book, open it and place the pattern in the centre of the fold. Using the needle pierce each hole. Be sure the needle comes out on the fold.

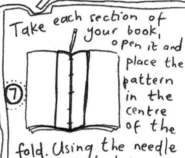

7

8

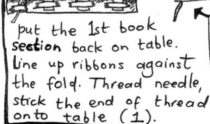

1

put the 1st book **section** back on table. Line up ribbons against the fold. Thread needle, stick the end of thread onto table (1).

Push needle through first hole, bring out through second hole and continue until you complete the section.

place 2nd section to on top of the first. Continue sewing as before. At the end take the loose starting thread (1) and tie onto the thread (2)

(2)

(2)

9.

Once the knot is secure place the 3rd section on top. When you have stitched this section stop at the end.

10.

Kettle stitch

Rather than moving up to the next section, thread the cotton through the stitch below it pull it to secure. Do this at the end of each section.

11.

Once all of the sections are complete finish off with a Double Kettle Stitch. Remove masking tape. Taa-daa! This is your book block gorgeousness Journal.

Now to add the cover ♡

12.

Get your chosen end papers and fold them in half. Carefully glue down the top fold.

← glue here and here ↓

14. Squash journal under a pile of books and leave for several hours.

Encyclopedia ☺

← Journal

13. Stick your end papers on each end of your book.

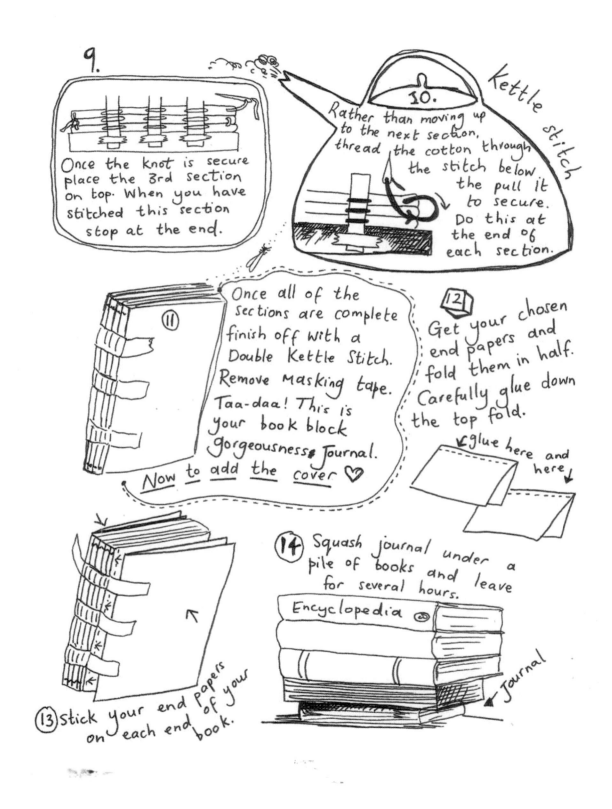

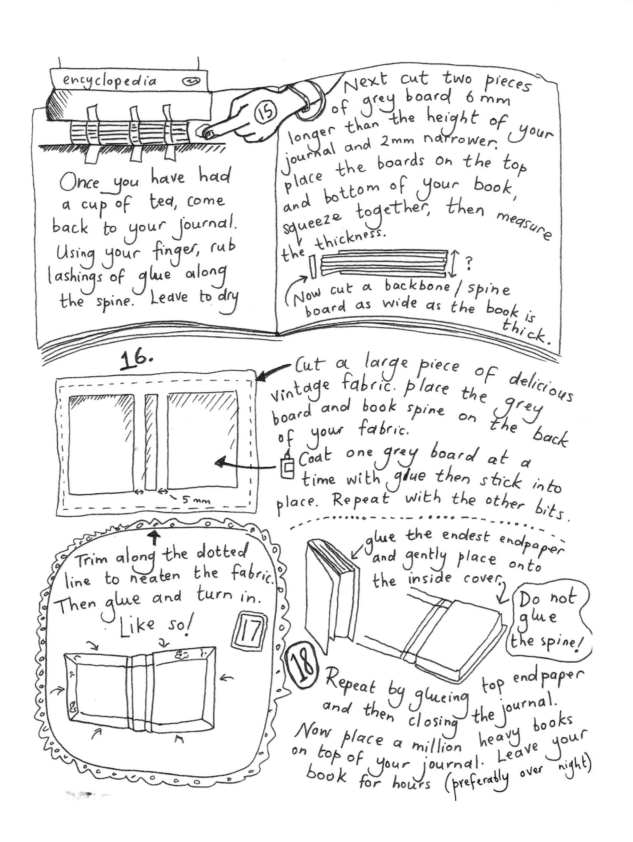

encyclopedia

Once you have had a cup of tea, come back to your journal. Using your finger, rub lashings of glue along the spine. Leave to dry

15

Next cut two pieces of grey board 6 mm longer than the height of your journal and 2mm narrower. place the boards on the top and bottom of your book, squeeze together, then measure the thickness.

Now cut a backbone / spine board as wide as the book is thick.

16.

5 mm

Cut a large piece of delicious vintage fabric. place the grey board and book spine on the back of your fabric.

Coat one grey board at a time with glue then stick into place. Repeat with the other bits.

Trim along the dotted line to neaten the fabric. Then glue and turn in. Like so!

17

glue the endest endpaper and gently place onto the inside cover.

Do not glue the spine!

18

Repeat by glueing top endpaper and then closing the journal. Now place a million heavy books on top of your journal. Leave your book for hours (preferably over night)

It is no coincidence that the words journal and journey start with the same four letters.

jour = French word meaning "day" ☼

I promise that through playing and interacting with your journal, a new pathway of gorgeousness WILL open up in your life.

Once you feel comfortable exploring your own gorgeousness in the pages of your journal, you can then take it further by actively acknowledging the gorgeousness in the world ➜

An exploration

Take your gorgeousness out for coffee
(or tea)

You will need these things:-

purse with coffee money

Journal or note pad

pencil or pen

some sunglasses

An open mind.

and then

find a delicious cáfe perfectly situated for people watching. The inner judge ♡loves♡ to look at people and ⚡snipe⚡. To help us grow beyond judgement & cultivate gorgeous perspectives we can learn to actively look for the gorgeousness in the world. Here's how:-

• Order latte, coffee, lapsang souchong or whatever
• Put on your sunglasses • Open journal / pad
• Chew pen. People watch. • Note all diversity, beauty, interesting parts and unique-ness in every person you see.

Vintage loving ♡

Seeing the gorgeousness can sometimes take patience and a special sort of looking. This looking is subtle. Sometimes it will be

But the gorgeousness will be there

the tangiable vintage love of an old man and old lady as they both gaze out to cold October seas foaming on grey sand. It might be the brassy gleam of a random light fitting. To retrain our (focus) and see beyond cosmetic appearance to the gorgeousness beyond may take a leap of faith but once you jump the elegance, intelligence, sorrowful, creative, wonderous exquisiteness of humanity will catch you. It will take your breath away.

It takes gorgeous eyes to see the deeper gorgeousness.

Remember...

You can choose to use gorgeous eyes to see

you.

You can begin here →

Look beyond your
body.
Who are you when all
roles, possessions, ideas
& false identities
are stripped away?

Just feel the answer,
thats all.

No one has ever come to this Experience called life with your rare, vibrant combination of love, adventure, shyness, beauty, beliefs, wisdoms, daydreams, humour, truth, Vision, hope, playfulness, viewpoint, Voice, understandings or gifts..

Your energy —
your you-ness IS
your gorgeousness!

You can unleash it like
champagne onto your
life & the world.

Say "yes" to yourself,
open your eyes to
Yourself and you
will realise that
you are already

Everything

You long to be.
& You are you!

What do you
love?
What do you
dream of?
What has you
overflowing with
deliciousness?

Document your loves

Collect, list and experiment with all the things you love.

Gather people, things, objects & activities that delight you.

Become an **icon** of what you believe in.

Celebrate what you feel to be *gorgeous*.

Circle the qualities that speak to your you-ness.

excellence

Quality   health   strength

Appreciation

Respect   purposefulness

kindness   Dignity   peace

Love

support

Commitment

play

Connectedness   truth

fairness   fun   honesty   Friendship

authenticity

Justice   Creativity

integrity   collaboration   freedom

trust   partnership

adventure   Compassion   inovation

spirituality

103

Consider all of your positive
body labels, the things you
love and are drawn to, the
qualities that mean everything to you.

Here are the seeds
of your gorgeousness!

The truth is that *you* — your
True Energy — is indescribable.
We know it is there because
of what you are touched
by, attracted to, delighted by.

Breathe your self in.

You. Are. Amazing.

As your natural, wild gorgeousness starts to emerge your energy levels will soar. The question now is:- what shall I do with this mysterious, empowered energy? How do I pour my new found gorgeousness into the world?

I (Love) this question!!!!

You see, for the last 18 years I tortured myself by trying to do, be, create, write and make art which would be "good enough"/publishable. Trying to give birth to these creations was labourious, squeezy, painful & uncomfortably frustrating. More often than not I was disappointed by my efforts. For so long

I doubted that I had any talent at all. My trouble stemmed from my lack of gorgeousness and essentially all of my attempts to be "published" were really just attempts to be loved.

Then one day I chose to stop resisting myself & instead just surrender to who I was.

When I decided to write this book I chose to do it in my own unique Bethan--ish sort of way. I decided to create something simply to delight myself. Every word has come from my heart-including the flaws. In fact I feel quite biblicaL about this piece of gorgeousness expression. I made it in 7 days. It is a declaration of my gorgeousness; shabby chic,

messy, funny, odd, historically blasphemous,
anti- Dictionary, some times hard to
understand, sometimes simple.

Some times what I've written may
make no real sense to anyone at
all, but it is gorgeous and <u>I</u> <u>love</u> <u>it</u>.

If you were to create something
in the image of your gorgeousness,
what would it be?

· A shop stuffed with exquisite items?
· Art made from finger painted butterflies?
· Cakes that connect friends whilst
whisking them to home- baked heaven?

·
. . . .
. . . .

(fill in your own expression
of gorgeousness)

You know how to create. You know your own form of self-indulgence. Practise it weekly, if not daily. Like Hansel and Gretal tracing breadcrumbs home in the moonlight, you can let your displays of You; your music, dancing, wave-watching, wood strolling, singing from your soul and stories of the heart lead you back to your Gorgeous Self. Following "shoulds," "musts" and "have to's" will take us to cages of our own making, but our joy, our pleasure, our radical self-expression will always lead us home again.

Buy yourself some charcole pencils, a box of cheap water colours or gather some sticks or shells. Begin a project; create something; do it for your eyes only. Give yourself permission to make mistakes; just let your self unfold naturally.

There is a vitality, a life
force, an energy, a quickening,
that is translated through you
into action, and because there
is only one of you in all time,
this expression is unique.
And if you block it, it will
never exist through any other
medium and will be lost.

— Martha Graham

Use these pages to capture what you would do if you no longer had to worry about your body.

If I were truly beautiful, I would....

If I fell in love with my body, I would stop....

If I completely trusted in my gorgeousness I'd no longer worry about...

If I stopped worrying about my appearance, I would finally be able to...

If I released my need for body perfection and instead focused on doing the things that delight me, I .....

For half an hour every day, sit, stand, walk, breathe, laugh, act and play as if you were the most gorgeous woman you could dream of being.

nurturing
the
growth

The purpose of this chapter is to connect you with support & resources to help you continue on the gorgeousness journey.

The New Place

Somewhere near the beginning of this book I said that "as women we need to create a new place for beauty to sit within our lives." This place may be different for each of us.

For (me) the new place is this:-

"Beauty can be measured by what it is expressing in the world. Beauty is <u>no longer</u> a veneer to be laid on from the outside. Beauty is <u>now</u> the true and natural outcome of what lies beneath. It is <u>not</u> a thick coat of foundation that we are slapping on to cover our flaws and inadequacies. Beauty is a radical expression of the deepest, most gorgeous self."

The best thing about this new beauty is that it doesn't run out. It will not fade as you get older... quite the opposite in fact. The more you cultivate it, the more it grows.

And you have infinite supplies of the stuff. It's impossible to run out of your you-ness. You are officially a fountain of gorgeousness.

You are
your
greatest
source of
gorgeousness.

To discover more about how the Dangling Carrot of Ideal Beauty influences our lives, I would recommend these books & websites:-

www.bethanstritton.com

 www.dove.co.uk (dove campaign for Real Beauty)

www.Anybody.squarespace.com (Anybody's Vent)

BODIES - Susie Orbach

The Beauty Myth - Naomi Wolf

Truth or Dare - Starhawk

The Media & Body Image: If Looks Could Kill - Dr. Maggie Wykes & Prof. Barrie Gunter

- Unbearable Weight: Feminism, western culture, and the Body - Susan Bordo
- Perfect Girls, Starving Daughters - Courtney Martin

And for books of pure inspiration....

- Women Who Run With ~~the~~ The Wolves - by Clarissa Pinkola Estes
- The Color Purple - by Alice Walker
- The Fat Black Woman's Poems - by Grace Nichols
- The Artist's Way - by Julia Cameron
- Homecoming: Reclaiming & Championing Your Inner Child - by John Bradshaw

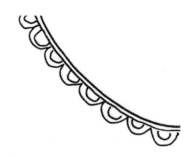

We are stardust.

We are golden.

And we've got to

get ourselves back

to the garden.

— Joni Mitchell
Woodstock

121

inspirational snippets
from women of
gorgeousness (you could
cut these out and place them in
strategic spots for yourself — or others —
to see).

No person is your friend who demands
your silence, or denies your right to
grow & be perceived as fully blossomed
as you were intended. — Alice Walker

"We don't see things as they
are, we see things as we are."
— Anaïs Nin

"We will discover the nature of our particular genius when we stop trying to conform to our own or to other people's models, learn how to be ourselves and allow our natural channel to open." – **Shakti Gawain**

"I'd rather have roses on my table, than diamonds on my neck." – Emma Goldman

"Here in this body are the sacred rivers: here are the sun and moon as well as all the pilgrimage places... I have not encountered another temple as blissful as my own body." – Sardha

Since you are like no other (person) being ever created since the beginning of time, you are incomparable. – Brenda Ueland

123

Glossary of terms

Gorgeousness:

the next evolution in Womankind's empowerment.
A process in which someone can stop trying to
fit an externally enforced mould of beauty and
invent their own version, based on who they are, instead.

The Dangling Carrot of Ideal Beauty

the card board cut out version of "ideal
female beauty" held up by an increasingly large
global community.

The Beauty Sellers

the companies and organisations who benefit
from the current beauty paradigm, for example;
the diet industry, fashion industry, beauty industry,
cosmetic surgeons, etc.

Enquiry

a tool that helps users to connect with
their deep feelings and "body" language
whilst by-passing the logical thinking mind
(hence releasing trapped feelings rather than suppressing them).

124

Ideal Beauty Conversation

the perpetual on-going media communication that encourages women to aspire to the Dangling Carrot Ideal. found predominantly in TV, films, female conversation & celeb magazines.

Expressionism

dynamic, colourful & emotion-charged, Expressionism was germany's contribution to modern art. I like to use this term to describe how we can deliver our truth to the world in a way that is raw, beautiful & an honest representation of who we are.(This book is Expressionism).

Transformationable

the ability we each have to change our experience of a situation, however bad or overpowering.

Atlantis

according to the classical greek philosopher plato, Atlantis was an ancient island that sunk into the sea. It was supposedly home to an advanced civilization who lived in abundance, spiritual wealth and prosperity.

Afterword

At the start of this book I said that there is no end product to this journey. Growing our own Gorgeousness is a path that we embark upon by re-membering and becoming vibrantly present to our selves. Gorgeousness sprouts in the sudden understanding that we are already "there". You will know when this hits you because you may feel the urge to jump wildly around your home or kiss strangers. This feeling may not last long, but by keeping on the path to Gorgeousness, it _will_ return...next time more wildly, deeper and just as delicious. Keep feeling for it.

There will be some days on our journey when Gorgeousness evades us. There will be times when we feel bloated with our own inadequacies and our thoughts will scurry with self doubt. On these days our dreams may feel futile; we will wonder who on earth we are kidding. These are fragile moments and we must treat ourselves kindly. These are times when we must love ourselves deeper and more soothingly than ever before; lie in a hot bath by candle light; curl under a blanket and read old novels; rock in a chair by the window while it rains outside; make bread; make soup; make calls to old friends. Like the tides and the seasons, Gorgeousness will ebb; it will flow. The more we live these moments, the more we will learn to stop pushing ourselves so hard. It's OK to stop! It's OK to rest. It's ok to put aside our goals and visions and projects if our souls are calling for gentle-ness instead.

Our job as re-covering carrot cultivators is simply to continue growing our own little patch of Gorgeousness until we are nourished, glowing and healthsome. It is the constant raking, digging, soothing, expressing, resting, supporting, embracing and trusting of our Selves that is the root vegetable of all happiness and self sufficiency.

Other books by bethan.

Unleash the
zoo in you

mango marmalade- a
gratitude journal

available from
bethanstritton.com

Notes

Notes

Notes

Notes

Notes

Notes

Notes

Notes

Notes

Notes